Third Eye on the Prize

poems by

Debra Sansone

Finishing Line Press
Georgetown, Kentucky

Third Eye on the Prize

For Grace and Lucy

Copyright © 2020 by Debra Sansone
ISBN 978-1-64662-314-3 First Edition
All rights reserved under International and Pan-American Copyright Conventions.
No part of this book may be reproduced in any manner whatsoever without written
permission from the publisher, except in the case of brief quotations embodied in
critical articles and reviews.

ACKNOWLEDGMENTS

*Aum Shanti Aum
with gratitude to Tapasviji,
my spiritual teacher*

Publisher: Leah Maines
Editor: Christen Kincaid
Cover Art and Design: Debra Sansone
Author Photo: Debra Sansone

Order online: www.finishinglinepress.com

Author inquiries and mail orders:
Finishing Line Press
P. O. Box 1626
Georgetown, Kentucky 40324
U. S. A.

Table of Contents

Iris 1

Found Poem: *For Matisse* 2

Bee Yoga 3

Three Mothers in Your Head 4

Remembering Frogs after Dark 5

Light Bird 6

Seaside Psalm 7

Hiccups and Interstices 8

Left Hand Release 9

Back Seat Baby Boomer 10

The Soul of a Teacher 11

First Intensive 13

Nuclear Family Test Ban Entreaty 14

Body Talks to Mind 17

Repair 18

The Ferocious Joy of Birdsong 19

Salty Wet Poem 20

Morning Night 21

Special Delivery 22

Perfect Man 23

Red-Tailed Ballet 24

Elephant Song 25

Where Two or More are Gathered 26

Color Lesson 28

Yoga in a Time of Climate Change 29

"You are a focal point where the universe is becoming conscious of itself."

—Eckhart Tolle

Iris

the pupil is a cipher
doorway to vision
exquisitely attuned
sentinel of photons
and desire

my daughter's cat
taught me this
sitting contentedly
by the window
turning his gaze

upwards toward
the overcast sky
still bright enough
to shrink his pupils
from circle to almond sliver

they plumped out again
when he turned his head
back toward the inane
shadows of manmade
shelter and boredom

until a bird flurried by a flash
of feathers whipping Whiskey's head
around to follow the whooshing whir
of wings like lightning
his attention now ignited

by intention and though
the light had not changed
iris and pupil were suddenly
servants of desire agreeing to open
fully to the promise of pursuit

Found Poem: *For Matisse*

I once dove into a perfectly flat, bottomless tray
of aquamarine
inhabited by turpentine traces
on duck
and emerged out of a peace of sea.

Henri was a lover grand, wheelchair notwithstanding;
he held a baton of amazement
that to him was just another labor of light.

I want to breathe a lassitude
of lavender
that resonates against a field of oyster vellum,
punctuated by a black hole of India ink.

Bee Yoga

Breath is the queen
indispensable and supreme
the One without whom
the hive would perish

The asanas are strong numerous
diligent drones and worker bees
powerful but interchangeable
their only value: service to the queen

Three Mothers in Your Head

A triumvirate of membranes
envelop your nervous system's core
meninges surrounding brain and spinal
cord each one a meninx *sounds like meanings*

outermost is dura mater *hard mother*
badass protector of the priceless
I will *not* tolerate your laying waste
to your talents don't even think about it

arachnoid mater is the *mother in the middle*
a delicate spiderweb of filaments she balances
juggles negotiates an endless stream of signals
and demands it's for your own good you know

and the deepest one pia mater *tender mother*
innermost highly vascular never take a break
cushion of cerebrospinal fluid
inseparable from that which she protects

the members of this triple guard
tenuously tethered together
mothering too important and difficult a job
for any one to do alone

Remembering Frogs after Dark

Sighing ageless lovers sing endlessly
more than a looping swallow swooping dirge
the time is high and hides its rhyme

Silent cave dwellers swell to fill a vast space
so that no matter where the sound may lead
altogether too many come rushing to be counted

We know of a young one catching seeds that twirl
and anyone who remembers must say *I will call it out*
as if a boundless promise spins and spins away

Light Bird

for twenty-seven moments
two sweeping arcs of light

born of reflections the sun
planted in the windowpanes

had an encounter with my living
room wall the strewn solar seeds

commanding a fleeting display
of form momentarily frozen

in a gesture representing 'bird'
reduced to elegant luminous lines

showing the sign for swooping
like the ones that once

lived in the sky
of my childhood drawings

Seaside Psalm

The ocean feels like infinity
as if I could ever know
what that resembles

it's the overpowering
sound of it sitting there
at the edge especially at night

so vast deep and unknowable
pulling us into its cold colossal
watery magnetic field

we tiny beings of 37 trillion cells
give or take 15 to 50 trillion
and a hundred billion neurons

remarkable even at our most stupid
frolicking at the hem of her salty skirt daring
to dip a toe or two into the power cresting on the sand

some venture further crazy bastards
diving deep without a tank seeking something
an extreme experience maybe enlightenment

and others willingly undergo
submersion to a depth
of life-threatening pressure for what

to see something to find out something
the most treasured most coveted
exclusive expensive land on earth

is that which touches it why because
it is our ancient primal mother
we climbed crawled clawed our way

out of her boundless body to find something
gills transforming oh so gradually
into lungs cell by cell

Hiccups and Interstices

Charlie died a year ago. A note to call his wife sat on the dry erase board propped on my work table; another reminder, a sticky note stuck to the butcher block, simply said, "Darling" with a phone number. My husband wondered aloud who "Darling" was. *Why did I follow through on this day?*

She answered after three rings, no machine, said she couldn't place my face, though they were guests at our wedding twenty years ago. In spite of that, her words poured out: how he didn't complain, through so many indignities. She described the contraption, like a hammock with straps and pulleys, that enabled her to move Charlie's gangly bulk from room to room when he was no longer ambulatory, to navigate the single step down into the living room of their split-level house. The first time he was lowered into it, Charles quipped, "This is the closest I'll ever get to Six Flags." She shared with me that he told her he was afraid of death; or, that he didn't want to die. But as the sound waves of our conversation passed over the phone line, he sent me a different message. We were eating lunch again, laughing, guffawing even. He was relating the dream he'd had about my anal retentive boss, Bill, whose bald head, in the dream, was completely covered with blue ink from the printing press in the college basement, the same one on which Charlie had printed my wedding invitations. That wasn't part of the dream, it really happened. Then MaryLynn dared to ask, "Are you the same one who would wake in the night, screaming?," and I said, "Yes." And when she asked, instead of feeling embarrassment or shame, I laughed and marveled at this question being asked of me now, when I had no memory of having shared that with my friend. But I'm not surprised that I did.

Later that night I go to a loft space where eight women dance and my knees carry the burden of bridging the truth in my hips, roots wanting to extend down through the bottoms of my feet. I make a note to revisit the poem I wrote about Charlie and ungrounded lightning bolts seeking release into the earth.

Left Hand Release

deep down in what feels
like an unreachable place
a nerve clamors for attention

sending up flares
like a crazy stoned bastard
with his pants on fire

streaking here and there
darting back and forth
constantly inconstant

now in the junction
where thumb meets wrist
then floating somewhere

off-center in the rib cage
persistently insistent
taunting appearing

then disappearing
here I am yoo-hoo
over here gotcha

it says you need me
as much as you need
to be rid of me

Back Seat Baby Boomer

standing up in the back seat
relic of another time still small
enough to drape my arms around
my father's neck as he drove

laugh at his silly comments
laugh at his laughing our
laughing unadulterated love
and freedom before braces

before breasts or blemishes
before my beloved cat taken
down by a car right out in front
the dreadful news delivered

by the kindly woman in the
burgundy house across the street
Dad! the first thing I screamed
as I tore out back to find him

even though he drove fast
I was never afraid at least
not in the car but at night
in dreams he would leave

or fly away or be taken
by a fire or accident or some
mythic darkness might stalk
in at any time and persist

the back seat was motion
air sunlight the open rolling
road of American promise
and post-war privilege

all our doubts worries and fears
left at home with my mother
whose job it was to catalogue
tend and preserve them

The Soul of a Teacher

To the ones who
lift up their charges
who never stop

until they see
at least a semblance
of a spark

in the eyes
of those
they serve

who soldier on
until the light
of recognition

is lit
in the minds
of those little lambs

even or especially
when those lambs
are big or old or lame

you are the ones
who chose this way
to spend your days

and nights and weekends
imparting elucidating
prodding and reframing

I lift my glass
to you because
you move us all forward

First Intensive

I sat on a sofa in the large main room, where we had faced each other in response to the query, *Tell me who you are.* It was early morning, no one else in the house yet arisen. There'd been three days of unceasing rain: torrents alternating with mist, once an outright storm sending electricity that challenged us to reach down and find our own power, let it ground into the earth. On this morning, our last before leaving, the clear sky and sun simply said, *we told you we'd be back.*

The white moon rested in the blue morning sky. In my monthly cycle, I felt her as a reassuring presence and sisterly guide. Earlier, I'd been out walking; each day, we contemplated while walking. I'd heard a birdsong: two notes repeated, simple, clear. I whistled those same two notes, twice repeating the pattern, and a few moments later, a bird—*was it the same one or another?*—sang it, and the pitch was exactly the same.

I kept walking, reaching a place near the house, but down a shallow slope. Feeling the presence of a red-haired woman who had something to teach me, I knew it was something I'd have to fall into, to fall down and receive whatever it was mother has to give, or not give, with all the other things attached that we may or may not want. *But how to separate them?* I stood there before a sapling, delicate and graceful. I hugged it, not what you may be thinking about hippie tree-huggers. A spontaneous embrace.

Afterward, I fell. *Here it is, the falling.* The leaves were damp on top, wet underneath from all those days of rain. Before, I would have resisted that wetness and the first sensation of cold that accompanied it, but now I lay down, back against the blanket of damp leaves, and beneath them, mother earth; and she held me strong. The coolness gave way to warmth, tears flowed, and they were warm, and the sun was warm, and I was warm.

Nuclear Family Test Ban Entreaty

did you have a nuclear family? I did

fission fusion mushroom cloud
stand your ground and say it loud
spinning electrons protons neutrons
now there's all kinds of crazy other ones

quarks of six flavors:
up and down
top and bottom
charm and strange

leptons mesons pions and hadrons
what's the matter no one told us
about the brains behind atoms
and molecules

but each of these has
a counterpart apparently
its anti-self which carries
the opposite charge

my house was full of dark matter
and plenty of dark energy too

gravity electromagnetism
weak and strong: the four forces
mind-bending spin
or spin bending mind

looping current
rotating platforms
does a graviton exist
what are sparticles

turns out supersymmetric particles
sleptons squarks selectrons
photinos gluinos winos and zinos
not to mention neutralinos and gravitinos

if you think you're a WIMP you're wrong
it's a weakly interacting massive particle

everything's got
electromagnetic force
colliding
with everything else

there are hyperons and baryons
neutrinos muons a heavy kind
of electron and tau rhymes with saw
weak forces and fermions

gravitons bosons W Z and Higgs
photons gluons of zero mass
those are fast
speed-of-light fast

then there are mesons born
when a quark and antiquark get it on

he used to say to me you're so negative
I should have said so are you and everybody
else and positive too and we'll all be
spinning around like this forever

until we're not

in the world of antimatter
antielectron is a positron

we might be here only because
moments after the Big Bang
one percent more muons
than antimuons formed

r e a l l y ? ? ?

remember nuclear testing way out
in the desert all those hapless
observers just standing there
getting their retinas fried

fascinating taboo like government
secrets don't look at the eclipse
crouch down and cover your head
in the school hallway

David Glowacki was standing
nearest to the light switch
his right middle finger brushed
across the cinder block wall

flipping it off
at the teacher's command
to immerse us
in semi-darkness

now we've split apart
endlessly by mutation
into countless subdivisions
and permutations

there's only one way
that I can see
to manage this, people
…embrace the weird!

make your mysterious ancestors proud

be the chameleon particle

Body Talks to Mind

I don't trust you to protect me
your judgement is faulty
if I leave it up to you you're likely
to hurt me pushing too hard
or running scared and avoiding me
altogether at least major parts
not to mention the whole
of me my integrity

I'm trying to get your attention
here so we can work together
and be integrated but you keep
wanting to split off and fragment
wrongly believing you have
all the answers

you do have the advantage
of proximity to mouth
language expression articulation
you two share the head where
eyes ears nose and tongue
reside so you try to monopolize
(almost all) the senses control
interpret put your spin
on whatever comes in filter
evaluate compartmentalize

but at least I have
the enveloping power of touch
clairvoyant organ of the skin
covering me from head to toe
palms fingertips soles of the feet
nerve endings strokes caresses
slaps taps quivers shivers
gooseflesh warm and cool
pain and pleasure itches
scratches and tickles

at least I have all that

Repair

The day was wet and verdant. We were to drive to the orthopedist's for a routine check-up six months after my daughter's reconstructive surgery for a torn ACL. The left knee it was, same one her grandmother had just had replaced. The left side of the body is the heart side. I picked her up from the high school where she was already waiting in the lobby. About to embark on the next phase of her life, she made a stunning picture wherever she walked: tall, strawberry blonde, projecting composure.

He really did a lovely job, the surgeon—her scar is small and straight. My mother's is raw, jagged, new. The wounds are different, thankfully. There has been a leaching of toxins, a large, long wave of transformations. After much time passes, miracles do happen. We're just begrudging about calling them that when they're not instantaneous.

The visit with Dr. Nissen was inconsequential. Soon they'll do a stress test, ask her to jump and run, compare her right and left extremities, assess her balance. He tried to extend warnings that would follow her after we left and continue his influence, but the cutting is long past, and he knows she has already decided to ignore his admonitions, and that she will be fine and strong.

On the way home, I began, inexplicably, to talk about alterations in a person's life course that happen when someone you're involved with goes somewhere, and you just follow, with no idea why or how you'll manage it. I told her for the first time about a boyfriend I'd had before I met her father, whom I'd followed to a little town in Massachusetts from New York City. The words came easily, this disclosure feeling new between us, like the light green leaves emerging all across the landscape.

The Ferocious Joy of Birdsong

One of the most dauntless forces imaginable
a mother bear's ferocity when her cubs are threatened
let me call up that strength so that my heart can open
without fear Abhaya right hand held up extended outward
in the same gesture we use when swearing to tell the truth

On an exquisite fall day warm with soft light remnant
of summer breeze momentarily abated my birds
serenade me in a chorus from the backyard trees
they sing in counterpoint to traces of wind that rustle
the leaves in rising swells and receding airwaves

enthusiastically jazzed they sound like an excited throng
of shoppers on sale day or a crowd awaiting the imminent
arrival of an adored celebrity they step on each other's lines
with abandon carry each other along on a wave of chirping
there's no end or beginning to their song

behind them a distant drone of highway traffic annoys me
but they continue as if unaware of disturbances in their field
riding the cadences with mother bear's ferocity Abhaya's
in there somewhere we'll go on singing we're not intimidated
we're not threatened we don't even know what that means

Salty Wet Poem

the ocean in me
has to go somewhere

will it bother you
if copious tears flow
while we copulate
if perchance
they pour forth
from my eyeballs
while your balls
slap my backside
from beneath
in the rhythm
of the waves

will that bring you
consternation
will it make you
wonder why
will you look for signs
of disturbance

there's no need really
it's just salt water
three-quarters
of the earth
three-quarters
of my body
and yours too

why are you
men so afraid
of the salt water

w h y n o t
j u s t t r y
 f l o a t i n g

Morning Night

when it's cloudy
I call it morning night
my daughter says

as we stand beneath
a clear September sky
waiting for the yellow bus

we track the height
and angle
of sun and moon

before turning to gauge
the length of our shadows
on the sidewalk

the bracing air of early autumn
raises the skin on our arms
into gooseflesh

Special Delivery

pain was a messenger
I tried to turn away
dreading what she brought
in a sealed parcel held
with strong gloved hands
against the bitter wind

my name was on it
clearly marked but surely
there must be a mistake
perhaps the wrong house
please check again

I tried dissuading her
sensing that what she
carried would find its way
to nerves too raw to touch

this package arrived
when I was home alone
expecting someone else
the icy blast that entered
when I opened the door
the cold that clung
to her garments caught
in my throat when I asked
what is it that you want

just sign here she said
if you are the one
so named to prove
that you have received
these contents

Perfect Man

Imagine

Sean Connery's accent
Brad Pitt's hair
Charlie Puth's vibrato
Cary Grant's cleft chin
Paul Newman's eyes
Ryan Gosling's smirk

whew

Trevor Noah's intelligent humor (and dimples)
Stephen Hawking's startling brilliance
the Dalai Lama's magnanimity
Yanis Varoufakis' conviction
Mr. Rogers' kindness'
Bryan Cranston's devilishness

Channing Tatum's chest arms ass

and the net worth of Jeff Bezos

yeah

Red-Tailed Ballet

seven minutes ago pulling into the parking lot
of Wade's Farm Fresh I looked up and noticed
two red-tailed hawks paired in a soaring air dance
circling in broad looping phantom arcs 'til
one suddenly vanished in a periwinkle puff

leaving the other to finish the piece solo
and grabbing the moment she commanded
the stage of the bottomless blue sky
climbing in an ever widening spiral
drawing a line of current with her path

a flying virtuoso the seconds without flapping
thrillingly extended stretching out 'til it seemed
she was propelled by an internal motor a high wire glider
meanwhile amidst this choreography two airplanes
crossed the sky within minutes of one another

their trajectory a mechanical steady-state
even from that distance strikingly different from and
inferior to that of the hawk and as I kept watching
this show another bird relieved itself on my windshield
the splat immediately crusting over on the sun-baked glass

and just like that sky came down to earth
lofty turned to squat ethereal became corporeal
reminding me to go do my shopping buy the vegetables
that when eaten will transform into the stuff of my body
then be expelled and transmogrified into something else

Elephant Song

Twilight rumblings rise and rise and rise
then ricochet off an invisible undulating
ceiling stretching across the savanna.

The pachyderms feel it in their wrinkled rough
skin in their muscles and nerves in their tendons
in the trunks they raise to trumpet

their song to all the other elephants.
Sound is their savior. In the density
of the forest sight and smell only take you

so far but the invisible temperature inversion
creates a duct along which sound is channeled
and provided there is little wind and turbulence

it carries all that they need—the herd—
to find enough to drink, adequate vegetation
and the wherewithal to nail the timing of their pairings

as infrequent as the opportunities are.
They are a lumbering monumental orchestra
delicately tuned to extremely low frequencies

able to detect remote vibrations that herald
the approach of distant storms
at the end of the dry season.

Where Two or More are Gathered

What eloquent Brit or Scot or Irish bard
witnessing the swelling shifting tsunami
of wings filling the sunset sky with swooping
gliding raving magnificence was first
to call it a *murmuration* of starlings

who christened the first *peep* of chickens or dubbed
a squawking spurt of color a *pandemonium* of parrots

was it a lyrical zoologist roaming linguist wayward shepherd
or drunken poet who stood on the plain as a thundering herd
approached and just before being crushed into oblivion
had the wherewithal to pull from his or her pocket a crumpled
bit of paper and scribble down the phrase a *crash* of rhinos

like God touching Adam fingertip to fingertip we christen
these feathered coteries baptize these beastly tribes

some ancient master of monikers deemed eagles too solemn
and fierce in the solitude of the hunt to gather for frivolous
socializing calling their meeting a *convocation* while larks
in elegance form an *exaltation* vain peacocks an *ostentation*
and swans circling a lake of blood a long-necked *lamentation*

emus may be a mindless *mob*
and pipers just a *poverty*

but so do human animals congregate in camaraderie
assemble in communion and are christened accordingly
a *hastiness* of cooks wields a flurry of blurry blades a sea
of consecrated habits swells to a *superfluity* of nuns while
waiting on the sidelines of worship a *bench* of bishops

perhaps this silver-tongued tribute of naming arises
from the unbridled power of collective creatures

the warm- and red-blooded Word forming and
informing scream of swifts *murder* of magpies
wake of buzzards *piteousness* of doves
butterflies a *rabble* effervescent babble
zeal of zebras *leap* of leopards!

Color Lesson

New baby shoots, before deepening in color, have a hue still filled with the light of the sun. Yellow is said to be the color of the third chakra, the solar plexus. In yoga it's referred to as the core or seat of our personal power, sometimes called the place of the shining gem. So what radiates out from our center? Immeasurable things.

The spectrum's abundant energy is apparent to any child with a new jumbo size box of Crayolas. The colors like brilliant fuchsia—not red or blue but both and something more—defy lines of demarcation. If forced to name the yellow-green crayon I'm holding now, most would call it green; but the yellow that nestles inside pushes out against the green, pulling it away from water toward light. The green of the heart chakra holds both a downward nod to earthiness and regeneration, and an upward tug toward blue sky and open endless atmosphere.

Soaring cannot happen without first bowing to the fire of the molten center.

Yoga in a Time of Climate Change

The wind today
is so ferocious
blowing too tame a word

it howls, but even that
feels too mild
a descriptor for this sound

wailing comes a little closer.
As we lie in savasana
surrendering on the mat

I think of air the heart's element
and the wailing sounds
like the Earth's heart

breaking in a spasm of torment
because her children
have lost their way.

Debra Sansone is a writer, artist, teacher, and healer. Her previous two volumes of poetry, *Shared Air and Other Poems* (2008), and *For Sky, Day is Night* (2013), were published by Finishing Line Press. Her first (unpublished) book of poetry was created at the age of fourteen and contained original photographs and artwork. Sansone is an alumna of Parsons School of Design and Harvard University. She has won national awards for her work in corporate training, multimedia production, and instructional design. She is the mother of two grown daughters, a devoted meditator, and sometime songwriter.

www.ingramcontent.com/pod-product-compliance
Lightning Source LLC
LaVergne TN
LVHW041509070426
835507LV00012B/1448